WHO KNEW?

WHO KNEW?

Revised and Updated

Things You Didn't Know About Things You Know Well

DAVID HOFFMAN

SHELTER HARBOR PRESS
NEW YORK

This revised edition published in 2016 by Shelter Harbor Press.

ISBN-13: 978-1-62795-061-9

Revised text copyright © 2016 by David Hoffman

Original book design by Holly Camerlinck
Revised book design by Igor Satanovsky

First edition published by Andrews McMeel in 2000

SHELTER HARBOR PRESS
603 West 115th Street, Suite 163
New York, N.Y. 10025
Info@shelterharborpress.com

Printed and bound in the U.S.A.

10987654321

For Dr. Bobby
Who knew none of this,
yet still managed
to know a lot

If Jell-O is hooked up to an EEG, it registers movements virtually identical to the brain waves of a healthy adult.

The original Twinkie filling was banana; it was replaced by vanilla-flavored cream during World War II, when the United States experienced a banana shortage.

The Cleveland, Ohio warehouse that houses the inventory for online rare book retailer Zubal Books was, until 1993, a Hostess snack cakes factory. Many of the pipes in the building still contain a non-aerated, sugary sauce the color of motor oil, which, when whipped, transforms into signature (and, yes, still edible) Twinkie cream filling.

There are seven loops in the squiggle atop every Hostess cupcake.

There are approximately 1,750 Os in every can of SpaghettiOs.

There are 1,218 peanuts in a single twenty-eight-ounce jar of Jif peanut butter.

By the time a kid graduates from high school, he will have eaten 1,500 peanut butter sandwiches.

Peanut butter's high protein content draws moisture from your mouth — which is why, in the end, it always sticks to the roof of your mouth.

One hundred shares of McDonald's stock purchased for $2,250 when first offered in 1965 has grown to 74,360 shares worth approximately $7 million (as of market close on December 31, 2014).

The average wait time for a drive-thru meal at McDonald's is 2 minutes, 39 seconds.

The drive-through McDonald's in Slough, England (about twenty miles/thirty kilometers west of central London) is owned by Queen Elizabeth II. The Bath Road Retail Park, the shopping center where the branch of the fast food chain is located, is a part of the Queen's vast real estate portfolio.

One out of eight people in the United States has worked at McDonald's. Among the former employees who have asked "Would you like fries with that?" are amazon.com founder Jeff Bezos, James Franco, Pink, Rachel McAdams, Jay Leno, Sharon Stone, Shania Twain and Food Network chef Anne Burrell.

The three dots in the Domino's Pizza logo represent the company's first three locations; the original concept was that a dot would be added for each new store that opened — a plan that ran out of steam as fast as the design ran out of space (if the company had stuck to their original plan, the number of dots on the domino would now number just under 11,000).

Modern-day pizza was invented when Don Raffele Esposito, a restaurant owner in Naples, Italy, decided to layer a traditional flatbread with fresh tomatoes, mozzarella and basil — ingredients he chose because they were red, white, and green, the colors of the Italian flag.

In 1853, George Crum, the head chef at Moon's Lake House in Saratoga Springs, New York, was insulted when hotel guest Cornelius Vanderbilt, the well-known railroad tycoon, sent back his dish of French fries, demanding that they be cut thinner and fried longer. In anger, Crum decided to teach the commodore a lesson and shaved off paper-thin slices of potatoes, threw them into a tub of ice water, let them soak, and dropped them in a vat of boiling grease. When they came out curled and fried crisp, he sprinkled salt on them and sent the potatoes back to the Vanderbilt table. Crum was bowled over when the guests sent back their compliments and requested another order. Soon, "Saratoga Chips" (later to become simply "potato chips") were a featured item on the hotel's menu.

M&Ms owe their success to the United States military, which was hungry for a candy that could hold up in G.I.s' pockets and backpacks and could be eaten without their trigger fingers getting sticky.

During their 1982 world tour, Van Halen's standard concert contract included a now legendary rider that stated among the food provided in the backstage area would be a bowl of M&Ms, with "absolutely no brown ones." While the clause appeared to be the height of obnoxious rock star excess, it was actually a quick and clever way for the group — concerned about older venues not being able to safely accommodate the massive amounts of state-of-the-art staging, sound equipment and lighting that they were bringing — to determine if the promoter had (or had not) properly read (and honored) their agreement.

Life Savers got their signature shape by accident, when the machine employed to press out a standard circular mint malfunctioned, inadvertently punching a hole in each one.

The Hershey's Kiss got its name from the puckering sound made by the manufacturing equipment as chocolate was dropped onto the conveyor belt during the production process.

When soda was first marketed and available, the bottles were sealed with a cork; the sound of the cork being removed is how soda came to be known as "pop."

The Up in 7-Up is often attributed to the fact there was lithium carbonate in the original recipe (and was for twenty years) until the FDA banned its use in beer and soft drinks in 1948.

The design for the first corkscrew was inspired by a tool called a gun worm that was used to extract bullets stuck in rifles.

There are 87,000 possible drink combinations available at Starbucks, once you factor in options such as size, shots, syrups, hot, cold, wet, dry, blended ...

Robert Cade, a University of Florida physiology professor, was determined to create a liquid that could quickly replace body fluids lost due to physical exertion and hot weather, so he developed a sports drink and tested it on ten of his school's football players. The team — the Gators — posted a winning record that season, and, as a result, people took to calling Cade's concoction Gatorade.

In 1891, Philadelphia inventor James Henry Mitchell revolutionized the packaged cookie business by building an apparatus that could combine a hollow cookie crust with a fruit filling. The machinery was quickly bought by the Kennedy Biscuit Works in Boston, who had established the tradition of naming their cookies and crackers after towns in the immediate area. Since the company already had the Beacon Hill and the Brighton, this fruit-filled number was christened the Newton. And although it was originally manufactured with a range of jam centers, fig quickly proved to be the most popular; hence the cookie officially became known as the Fig Newton.

While making cookies for her hotel guests one evening in the late 1930s, Ruth Wakefield lacked the powdered cocoa called for in the recipe, so substituted tiny bits of chopped chocolate in its place. Unexpectedly, the chocolate pieces did not melt in baking, but, rather, held their shape, softening only slightly to a creamy texture. She served the cookies anyway, naming them Toll House after the inn she owned.

Besieged by customers' requests, Cleveland restaurant owner (and former chef at New York's Plaza Hotel) Hector Boiardi decided to bottle his famous spaghetti and meat sauce. With local success came an offer for national distribution, but, fearing that Americans would have trouble pronouncing (not to mention remembering) his Italian surname, he marketed and sold his tasty treat under the phonetic spelling, "Boy-ar-dee."

In 1880, the flour produced by the Washburn-Crosby Company, a Minnesota milling firm, took first place at an international exhibition held in Cincinnati. Sensing the public relations potential in their victory, company officials decided to start marketing their award-winning product under the name Gold Medal. But when an avalanche of mail poured in from housewives requesting recipes (or asking about baking problems), the men who ran Washburn-Crosby felt the responses they sent back should come from a woman. So Betty Crocker was born. The name Betty was picked because it was familiar and friendly; Crocker was chosen to honor William Crocker, a former director of the company.

Ben Cohen and Jerry Greenfield wanted to go into the bagel business, but when they discovered that the equipment alone would cost $40,000, the two opted to take a $5 correspondence course (offered by Penn State University) in ice cream making instead.

It takes about fifty licks to finish a single scoop ice cream cone.

Despite being available only three months a year, the Girl Scouts' Thin Mints rank third on a list of the best selling cookies in the United States (behind Oreo and Chips Ahoy).

Wedding cake was originally thrown at the bride and groom, instead of eaten by them.

A chef's hat is tall and balloons at the top so as to counteract the intense heat in the kitchen; the unique shape allows air to circulate around the scalp, keeping the head cool.

Before attending the Cordon Bleu and mastering the art of French cooking, Julia Child did intelligence work for the Office of Strategic Services in India and China during World War II.

The five interlocking Olympic rings are black, blue, red, white and yellow because at least one of them appears on every national flag.

The single best-selling item at Costco is Kirkland toilet paper; approximately one billion rolls are purchased annually.

If a penny is randomly tossed into the air, the odds are actually one percent higher that it will land on tails as opposed to heads. This is because the image of Lincoln on the heads side weighs more, which slightly increases the chance that it will end up on the bottom.

The penny is the only currently minted U.S. coin featuring a profile that faces to the right.

The dollar sign is believed to be a combination of the letters P and S, PS being the abbreviation for the Spanish peso, the principal coin in circulation in the United States until 1794, when we began marketing our own dollars.

The paper used to make money is composed of linen and several types of cotton, including scraps of denim — which gives it its unique, fabric-like feel and durability.

A million dollars in twenty dollar bills weighs 102 pounds.

Coin banks are commonly shaped like pigs because in the eighteenth century frugal people saved their money in earthenware jars made of dense, orange clay known as pygg.

It is only in the last ten years that the city of Rome has begun to collect the approximately $3,500 in change that is tossed into the Trevi Fountain on a daily basis — and only after it was learned that a homeless man was successfully (and regularly) stealing the stash from the water using a magnetized pole. All Italian coins and Euros end up in the coffers of the town council (most recently, they were used to subsidize a food bank); foreign currency is donated to the Red Cross.

A dime has 118 ridges around the edge.

A portrait of Franklin Delano Roosevelt appears on the dime because of his work on behalf of the March of Dimes and its battle against polio, the disease that crippled him.

Three of the first five U.S. Presidents — John Adams, Thomas Jefferson, and James Monroe — died on July 4th.

James Madison, the fourth President of the United States, stood only five feet four inches tall and weighed less than one hundred pounds.

In order to give it an even greater illusion of height, the Eiffel Tower in Paris, France, is painted in three variations of a single color, with the lightest shade at the top and the darkest at the bottom.

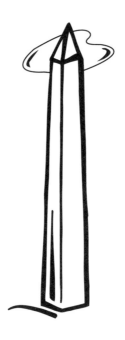

There is a noticeable change in color on the exterior of the Washington Monument (about one-third of the way up), because a lack of funds (and a twenty-five year halt in construction) meant three types of stone from two different quarries were used in the building process. While the two sections closely resembled each other on completion, over time, a combination of wind, rain, and erosion caused the marbles to weather differently, resulting in the inconsistency.

The Pentagon, one of the largest office buildings in the world, has twice as many bathrooms as is necessary, because when it was built Virginia laws still required separate toilet facilities for blacks and whites.

While his wife spent long hours posing for the figure, the model for the face of the Statue of Liberty was Charlotte Bartholdi, mother of the French sculptor Frédéric-Auguste Bartholdi, who designed it.

Portrait artist James Whistler decided to paint his mother when the person who had scheduled an appointment with him failed to show.

In 1961, Henri Matisse's *Le Bateau* ("The Boat") hung upside-down for forty-seven days at the Museum of Modern Art in New York City (and was seen by 116,000 visitors) before someone noticed the mistake.

The man who commissioned the
Mona Lisa refused it.

Leonardo DiCaprio was named after artist Leonardo da Vinci; apparently, his pregnant mother was standing in front of a Leonardo painting at the Uffizi Gallery in Florence, Italy, when she first felt DiCaprio kick.

The flashing warning light atop the Capital Records Tower in Hollywood also spells out H-O-L-L-Y-W-O-O-D in Morse code.

Sunglasses date back to fifteenth-century China, where they were worn by judges to conceal their expressions while presiding over court.

The idea of painting fingernails originated in China, where the color of someone's nails indicated their social rank.

Cosmetics company Avon got its name from Stratford-upon-Avon, since it was volumes of Shakespeare that company founder David McConnell first sold door-to-door. However, when the complimentary vial of perfume he gave to each housewife proved more popular than the books, a beauty products empire was born.

The kitchen dishwasher was invented by the socialite wife of an Illinois politician, not because she was fed up with the ho-hum chore of dirty dishes, but because she had had it with careless servants who too frequently broke her expensive china while washing it.

The microwave oven was born when an engineer testing a magnetron tube noticed that the radiation leaking from it had caused the chocolate bar in his pocket to melt.

The average American eats seventy-two frozen dinners a year.

Following the sales success of his disposable ballpoint pen in Europe, French businessman Marcel Bich was ready to take on the international market. He had named the product after himself, but realizing that Americans would incorrectly pronounce the name (spelled B-I-C-H) as *bitch*, he smartly dropped the 'H' and called his pen Bic.

A book of maps is called an atlas because early editions commonly featured a picture of Atlas, carrying the world on his shoulders, on the cover.

According to author L. Frank Baum, the name Oz was thought up when he looked at his filing cabinet and noticed one drawer marked A-G, a second tagged H-N, and a third labeled O-Z.

Wicked author Jeffrey Maguire chose Elphaba as the name of the Wicked Witch of the West in homage to Oz author L. Frank Baum. The name is a phonetic take on Baum's initials, L-F-B.

"Cinderella" has been made into a movie more times than any other story.

Shrek is Yiddish for monster.

Walt Disney's *Frozen* is inspired by Hans Christian Andersen's "The Snow Queen", and the names of four of the film's main characters — Hans, Kristoff, Anna and Sven — were intended (especially when spoken quickly, in that order) as a tribute to him.

It was the sight of Clark Gable peeling a raw carrot with a pen knife, then munching on it (as he attempted to teach Claudette Colbert how to hitchhike) in *It Happened One Night* that inspired Warner Brothers animator Bob Clampett to give Bugs Bunny his signature carrot chomp.

The sight of oranges in all three
The Godfather films signals that death
(or a close call) is about to happen.

Sixty-one scenes in *The Godfather* feature food or people eating.

Legally Blonde runs only ninety-six minutes, yet Reese Witherspoon sports forty different hairstyles.

According to the film's animators, you'll see 6,469,952 black spots every time you watch *101 Dalmatians*.

In *Pulp Fiction*, the word f**k is used 257 times.

In the early 1950s, author Ian Fleming would regularly commute from his home in Kent to his office in London. The bus he would take — #007 — would serve as inspiration for a novel he was working on about a secret service agent.

Martial arts actor Bruce Lee was so fast that many of his scenes had to be shot at 32 frames per second (rather than the normal 24 frames per second) in order to slow down the film so viewers could see his moves.

To make things easier while mixing the *American Graffiti* soundtrack, George Lucas and sound designer Walter Murch labeled all of the reels of film R and all of the dialogue tracks D, and then numbered each of them sequentially, starting with 1. When Murch later asked Lucas for Reel 2, Dialogue 2 — or more precisely, for R2, D2 — Lucas liked the way it sounded so much that he made a note of the name for another project he was writing.

Director Wes Craven named Freddy Krueger after a kid who bullied him in school.

The von Trapp family may have dramatically hiked over the Alps into Switzerland in the movie version of *The Sound of Music*, but in reality, they escaped by walking to the local train station and boarding the next train to Italy. Had they truly climbed every mountain, they would have ended up in Nazi Germany, near Hitler's mountaintop retreat.

Because the studio expected it to bomb, the budget of *Casablanca* was so low that the plane used in the background of the final scene was a small cardboard cutout. To give it the illusion of being full-size, the producers hired little people to portray the crew preparing it for take-off.

While inevitably linked to *The Graduate,* the song "Mrs. Robinson" was originally called "Mrs. Roosevelt" and had nothing to do with the plot of the film. Paul Simon had penned it as a tribute to Eleanor Roosevelt and days gone by, and it was only when director Mike Nichols begged him to contribute a new song to the movie's soundtrack that he changed the title.

The term "paparazzi" comes from Federico Fellini's *La Dolce Vita*. In the film, Marcello Mastroianni writes a gossip column and Walter Santesso plays his co-worker, a tabloid photographer named Paparazzo.

Melissa McCarthy based her character in *Bridesmaids* on Food Network star Guy Fieri.

Marilyn Monroe developed her signature walk by hacking off the heel of one shoe.

The signature line drawing of
Alfred Hitchcock's profile was drawn
by Alfred Hitchcock himself.

Hitchcock purchased the film rights to Robert Bloch's novel *Psycho* anonymously — and then proceeded to buy up as many copies of the book as he could in order to keep the ending a secret.

While Edward Hopper's *House by the Railroad* (1925) was the first oil painting by any artist to be acquired by the Museum of Modern Art, it is perhaps more recognizable as the inspiration for the Bates family home in *Psycho*. The use of light, the architectural style of the house, and the perspective in which it was drawn all mirror what is seen in the film.

Thanks to fast-buzzing wings, houseflies hum in the key of F.

Herrings communicate by farting.

The flatulence of a single sheep could power a small truck for 25 miles a day. Their digestive process produces methane gas, which can be burned as fuel.

Each instance of dog poop that goes un-scooped attracts approximately 144 flies.

Seeing eye dogs are trained to pee and poop on a spoken command (most commonly, "do your business"), so that their owners know when it is necessary to clean up after them.

The person responsible for bringing the first Akita to the United States was Helen Keller.

A lion's roar can be heard up to five miles away.

Tuna has a very strong smell and taste; as a result, many cats can become addicted to it. Veterinarians refer to them as "tuna junkies."

Every cat's nose pad is ridged in a pattern that is unique, similar to a human fingerprint.

Great white sharks can go three months without eating.

With no prior training (or even exposure), cockatoos are able to pick almost any lock.

Bulls are color blind and cannot see red. It is the bright color and motion of the cape that causes them to charge.

Lobsters show no visible signs of aging, but the do grow bigger and bigger until they die.

The female praying mantis chews off her partner's head during mating.

According to *The Old Farmer's Almanac*, the number of cricket chirps you count in a fourteen-second interval, plus forty, will tell you the current air temperature.

The original Volkswagen Beetle was commissioned by Adolph Hitler and designed by Ferdinand Porsche.

In the early 1920s, taxicab company owner John Hertz (who would later go on to start a rental car business) funded a University of Chicago study to determine which color in the spectrum was most visible from a far distance. When the answer came back "yellow," he had all of the cars in his fleet painted exactly that, beginning a tradition that would catch on nationwide, and carry over to school buses and traffic signs.

The name Jeep is derivative of the expression "G.P.," military slang for General Purpose Vehicle.

The modern day uniform for the Italian Air Force was designed by Giorgio Armani.

The first service uniform to be registered with the United States Patent and Trademark Office (Trademark # 0762884) was the Playboy Bunny outfit.

Nike's famed "Swoosh" logo was created in 1971 by Carolyn Davidson, a graphic design student at Portland State, who sketched it out on a piece of tissue paper and was paid thirty-five dollars for her effort. A dozen years later, Davidson would be given an undisclosed amount of stock for her contribution to the company's brand.

Nike's signature design came about when Phil Knight, a former runner at the University of Oregon, and Bill Bowman, his college coach, took a piece of rubber, stuck it into a waffle iron and crafted a crisscross-patterned sole that markedly increased traction.

The lunar landing suits that Neil Armstrong and Buzz Aldrin wore when they stepped off Apollo 11 and walked onto the moon were made by Playtex, the apparel company better known for manufacturing bras and women's undergarments.

The elastic strap with a clasp — created as a way to fasten any snug garment, but most commonly found on a bra — was invented by Mark Twain.

It takes two seconds for a properly trained Gap employee to fold a short sleeve t-shirt.

The Beach Boys toyed with calling themselves the Pendletons, figuring if they did, they would get free shirts.

The punk rock group the Ramones got their name from Paul Ramon, an early stage name used by Paul McCartney — and the pseudonym under which he would often check into hotels during the heyday of the Beatles.

The rock song with more cover versions than any other is Paul McCartney's "Yesterday," having been recorded by more than 3,000 different performers.

More than fifty famous musicians, often referred to as "the 27 Club," have died at the age of 27, including Jimi Hendrix, Amy Winehouse, Janis Joplin, Jim Morrison, and Kurt Cobain.

The first professionally produced album on which Jon Bon Jovi appeared was the 1980 Star Wars Christmas album called *Christmas in the Stars*. Billed under his birth name, John Bongiovi, he sang the lead vocals on "R2-D2 We Wish You A Merry Christmas."

The word "nerd" was coined by Dr. Seuss in his book *If I Ran the Zoo*.

The term "hanky panky" stems from a magician's practice of using a handkerchief in one hand to distract the audience from noticing what he is doing with the other.

X's symbolize kisses because in ancient days, when few people knew how to write, they would simply sign an X to show their agreement, then kiss the mark to emphasize their sincerity.

For centuries, it was customary at Irish weddings for a couple's clasped hands to be tied together by rope as a visual representation of their union, which could explain why, when two people get married, we say they are "tying the knot."

The military salute evolved from medieval times, when knights in armor would raise their visors to reveal their identities.

The football huddle was conceived by Paul Hubbard, a deaf quarterback at Gallaudet University in Washington, D.C., who used sign language to communicate. Not wanting the opposition to see his signals, the team would bunch together to shield him.

There are portions of Wisconsin that are further east than parts of Florida.

Maine is the only state whose name is just one syllable.

In terms of area, Juneau, Alaska (at 3,000 square miles) is the largest city in the United States, yet it can only be reached by boat or plane.

There really is a place called Podunk — and it's in East Brookfield, Massachusetts.

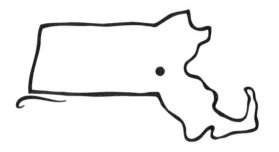

When Disneyland opened in 1955, its Tomorrowland area represented a city from 1986 (that year was selected because it would be the next scheduled appearance of Halley's Comet).

The gold decorating the exterior of It's A Small World at Disneyland isn't paint, but 22-karat gold leaf. And not just because it looks amazing; gold leaf is, over time, more cost-effective — since it does not need to be replaced as often.

People who work at Disneyland are never referred to as employees; rather, they are called "cast members." Cast members who work on It's a Small World refer to it as "the asylum," on the theory that that's where they'll end up as a result of repeated (over)exposure to the song.

Disneyland cast members who don a full body character costume (with head) and walk around the park are known as "fuzzies."

On average, the character costumes worn at Disneyland — and any other theme park — weigh forty pounds, and during the hot summer months, under the blazing sun and surrounded by crowds, the inside can heat up to 110°F.

To actually cook an egg, a sidewalk would have to be 158°F.

Joe Sheridan was closing up the restaurant at Ireland's Foynes Airport in 1945, when bad weather forced a transatlantic flight to turn around and come back. Realizing that the plane's passengers would be tired and irritable, Sheridan stayed late and greeted them with coffee that had been mixed with a little sugar, spiked with a shot of Irish Whiskey, and topped with freshly whipped cream. When asked if what they were drinking was Brazilian coffee, Sheridan replied, "No. It's Irish Coffee." The name stuck.

Over the last ten years, one of the top-selling items at airport newsstands across the country has been mechanical pencils. Chalk it up to the Sudoku phenomenon, the number of passengers who like to pass their flying time with the popular puzzles, and the simple fact that planes do not come equipped with pencil sharpeners.

It would take at least 411 years to spend one night in every hotel room in Las Vegas.

The TV remote control is the single dirtiest item in any given household, hospital, or hotel room.

The three-tone musical chime that identifies NBC is composed of three notes — G, E, and C — which is short for the company's original owner, General Electric Corporation.

In order for their skin to get a deep, dark (but not orange!) color, celebrity contestants on *Dancing with the Stars* undergo five layers of spray tan, followed by a hand-buffed stain, a bronzer, and a final dusting of glitter. The whole process takes about forty-five minutes.

In most TV commercials (and print advertisements), the hands on a watch are set at 10:10 because that arrangement draws attention to the logo and frames the manufacturer's name.

While filming *Star Trek*, director Joe Pevney asked Leonard Nimoy to improvise a hand sign to accompany Spock's Vulcan farewell, "Live long and prosper." The gesture Nimoy came up with — right hand lifted, palm facing out, with the fingers separated in a V-shape — is an obscure Rabbinical blessing Nimoy remembered from his youth.

An unbelievably rude waiter at Oscar's Tavern in New York City so unintentionally amused Muppet creator Jim Henson and *Sesame Street* director Jon Stone that he inspired the creation of Oscar the Grouch (who, by the way, was orange for the show's first season).

Big Bird's costume is made of 4,000 white turkey feathers, dyed yellow.

"The Rachel," the iconic haircut that became Jennifer Aniston's signature look on ten seasons of *Friends*, remains the most requested hair style of all time.

Aunt Harriet, the matriarch of "stately Wayne Manor," never existed in the comic book version of Batman but was created specifically for the 1960s TV series because producers feared that two bachelors (and a butler!) living together had homosexual overtones.

The only people to have appeared on *Saturday Night Live* as a cast member, host, and musical guest are Dan Aykroyd and Michael McKean (Aykroyd performed as part of The Blues Brothers; McKean sang and played bass with Spinal Tap).

One side of the couch that was in the Ricardos' living room on *I Love Lucy* was constructed with three inches of additional padding, so Desi Arnaz, when seated, would look taller than he actually was.

Lincoln Logs were invented by John Lloyd Wright, the son of Frank Lloyd Wright. He got the idea from a building technique his father had used in designing Tokyo's Imperial Hotel.

Silly Putty resulted from a failed World War II effort to develop an inexpensive synthetic substitute for rubber.

There are eighty-six coil turns (and sixty-three feet of wire) in a standard-size Slinky.

Play-Doh was originally formulated as a compound to clean wallpaper.

Barbie's last name is Roberts.

The smell of Crayola crayons is so familiar that it is one of the twenty most recognizable scents to American adults (ranking up there with coffee and peanut butter). The smell is so soothing that sniffing the crayons has been proven to lower blood pressure.

The Ouija Board got its name by combining the French and German words for "yes" — *oui* and *ja*.

The name Atari was chosen so that consumers would think that the Northern California-based company was Japanese.

The fifty-two playing cards in a typical deck represent the fifty-two weeks in a year; the four suits, the four seasons.

Six eight-stud Lego pieces can be combined 915,103,765 ways.

The Rubik's Cube can be twisted and turned into over 43 quintillion (43,252,003,274,489,856,000 to be exact) configurations in an attempt to solve the puzzle. The least amount of twists it takes to successfully line up one solid color on all six sides is twenty-two.

The thumbnails of every G.I. Joe are deliberately cast on the inside (as opposed to the outside) of the hand so as to give the action figure an easily identifiable characteristic that doubles as a trademark.

The total amount of money in a standard Monopoly game is $15,140; real money was slipped into packs of play money that were smuggled into POW camps inside Germany during World War II.

Military toilet paper is printed with a camouflage pattern, because standard-issue white could attract enemy fire at a very vulnerable time.

The inspiration for Post-It notes came to a 3M scientist not while on the job, but while singing in the church choir — and after the pieces of paper he used to mark his place in his hymnal repeatedly fell out.

The most distributed publication in the world is the IKEA catalog, with a current print run of more than 217 million copies a year.

The main character in Margret and H.A. Rey's children's book was a curious boy monkey named Fifi, until their publisher expressed doubts and they decided to call him George.

Dr. Seuss' first book, *And to Think That I Saw It on Mulberry Street* was rejected twenty-seven times — until one day, while walking down Madison Avenue in New York City, he ran into a former classmate who had just been named the juvenile department editor at a publishing house...

The interlocking "NY" logo, so identified with both New York City and the Yankees, was actually created by Louis B. Tiffany — for a medal to be given by the New York City Police.

The signature black mock turtlenecks worn by Steve Jobs were designed (specifically for him) by Issey Miyake.

When Google first began as a graduate school research project at Stanford in 1995, Larry Page and Sergey Brin called their search engine BackRub.

The 50-star American flag was designed by Robert Heft for a high school class project. His teacher originally gave him a B−, but promised he'd change the grade if the flag was accepted by Congress. (It was. He did.).

On average, we forget 80 percent of what we learn on any given day.

David Hoffman is a writer, producer, on-air correspondent and the author of fifteen books on popular culture. He lives in Los Angeles, where he likes to pretend all of this is hard work.